CHILDREN'S AUTHORS

GRACE LIN

Jill C. Wheeler
ABDO Publishing Company

visit us at
www.abdopublishing.com

Published by ABDO Publishing Company, 8000 West 78th Street, Edina, Minnesota 55439.
Copyright © 2012 by Abdo Consulting Group, Inc. International copyrights reserved in all
countries. No part of this book may be reproduced in any form without written permission from the
publisher. The Checkerboard Library™ is a trademark and logo of ABDO Publishing Company.

Printed in the United States of America, North Mankato, Minnesota.
062011
092011

 PRINTED ON RECYCLED PAPER

Cover Photo: photo courtesy of Grace Lin
Interior Photos: AP Images p. 9; photos courtesy of Grace Lin pp. 5, 7, 11, 12, 14, 17; *Ling &
    Ting*, Grace Lin, Little, Brown Books for Young Readers p. 19; *The Year of the Rat*, Grace Lin,
    Little, Brown Books for Young Readers p. 16; *Where the Mountain Meets the Moon*, Grace
    Lin, Little, Brown Books for Young Readers p. 21
Image on page 13: The Ugly Vegetables
                Text copyright © 1999 by Grace Lin
                Illustrations copyright © 1999 by Grace Lin
                Used with permission by Charlesbridge Publishing, Inc.
                All rights reserved.

Series Coordinator: Megan M. Gunderson
Editors: Tamara L. Britton, Megan M. Gunderson
Art Direction: Neil Klinepier

Library of Congress Cataloging-in-Publication Data

Wheeler, Jill C., 1964-
 Grace Lin / Jill C. Wheeler.
    p. cm. -- (Children's authors)
 Includes index.
 ISBN 978-1-61783-049-5
 1. Lin, Grace--Juvenile literature. 2. Authors, American--20th century--Biography--Juvenile
literature. 3. Illustrators--Biography--Juvenile literature. 4. Children's stories--Authorship--
Juvenile literature. I. Title.
 PS3562.I46774Z93 2011
 813'.6--dc22
 [B]
                                            2011011625

4562

CONTENTS

Dorothy's Not Chinese

Grace Lin remembers the excitement as her elementary school prepared a production of *The Wizard of Oz*. Like her classmates, Lin had dreams of playing Dorothy. Yet one day, those dreams were dashed by a friend's remark. She told Lin that Dorothy is not Chinese. Lin was crushed. She decided she would not even try out for the part.

For many years, Lin and her family were the only Asian family in her hometown. Most of the time, she tried to forget she was different. Still, she was reminded every time she looked in the mirror. Lin remembers being especially frustrated as a young reader. She loved to read. But she could rarely find quality stories with Asian main characters.

Today, Lin writes and illustrates her own books. She has published more than 20! Many feature kids just like she used to be. Lin has also illustrated books for other authors.

Lin did not set out to write **multicultural** stories. Yet in writing about her own life, she has touched the lives of multicultural readers.

In 2010, Lin's novel *Where the Mountain Meets the Moon* was named a **Newbery Honor Book**. Some reviewers have called the book a Chinese version of *The Wizard of Oz*. In Lin's world, it seems Dorothy can be Chinese after all.

Lin's Asian-American heritage has inspired many of her books.

A Love of Reading

Grace Lin was born on May 17, 1974. She grew up in a white, two-story house in New Hartford, New York. Grace's parents had moved to the United States from Taiwan, an island off the coast of China.

Grace's father, Jer-shang, was a doctor who cared for people with kidney diseases. Her mother, Lin-Lin, was trained as a **botanist**. They had three daughters. Grace's older sister is named Beatrice and her younger sister is named Alice.

Growing up, Grace's life at home was always a little different. For one thing, her family ate rice with chopsticks! But Grace was also much like her classmates. She watched *Little House on the Prairie* and learned American history.

Grace also loved to read. At home, she liked to curl up with a book by a large banana plant. The plant hid her from view. When her mother called for her to come clean her room, Grace could keep reading if she stayed tucked behind the big plant!

Grace (right) and her sisters all had Chinese nicknames. Grace was called Pacy after her Chinese name, Pai Se. Beatrice was called Lissy, and Alice was called Ki-Ki.

Grace pored over books by Carolyn Haywood and Maud Hart Lovelace. She also liked the Oz books, the Narnia series, and Noel Streatfeild's Shoes series. Grace loved Richard Scarry's books so much she traced the illustrations over and over again.

At the time, Grace did not seem to want to know about her heritage. But, she read the Chinese folktales her mother left lying around. Years later, Grace realized those books were her mother's way of sharing Chinese **culture** with her daughter.

Always an Illustrator

Grace considered becoming an illustrator even as a young girl. She thought it was fun to make books. In fact, she made books for any school project she could. Grace also realized that some people make books for a living.

However, Grace also dreamed of becoming an Olympic figure skater. During the summer, she drew pictures of herself twirling and dancing on ice. But when winter came, Grace fell every time she tried to lift her foot off the ice! She quickly realized she would have more success as an illustrator.

In seventh grade, Grace entered a contest for young writers and illustrators. She wrote her illustrated book, *Dandelion Story*, about flowers that talk to one another. Grace won fourth place and $1,000 to put toward her future education. When she was older, Grace learned who had won first place. It was Dav Pilkey, creator of the popular Captain Underpants series!

Readers love Dav Pilkey's humorous Captain Underpants series.

FINDING HER ART

After high school, Grace **enrolled** at the Rhode Island School of Design (RISD) in Providence. There, she studied children's book illustration. Grace knew her parents might be upset at her decision. They had hoped she would study science, like her sisters.

Yet, studying art proved to be just as difficult as science! One assignment required Grace to make a violin from cardboard without using glue or tape. This was challenging! But Grace did it with the help of many, many tabs that held everything together.

In 1995, Grace spent a term studying in Rome, Italy. There, she learned two important things. The first was that she knew more about Rome's history than she knew about her own **culture**'s history. Second, she learned to stop copying other artists and begin developing her own style.

Grace stopped using carefully mixed colors. Instead, she opened her tubes of paint and boldly used lots of it! Today, Grace is known for a painting style called **gouache**. She creates smooth, flawless, bold areas of color in her illustrations.

Today, Grace enjoys selling her work at RISD alumni sales.

The Magic of Ugly Vegetables

Lin graduated from RISD in 1996. She then worked for a while in a children's bookstore. She also attended workshops and conferences to learn more about the publishing industry. In addition, she sent thousands of color copies and postcards featuring her work to various publishers.

At first, no one seemed to pay attention. Lin managed to get by on the money she earned at the bookstore. She also got a job designing personalized gifts for a party

Lin and her mother in their own "ugly vegetable" garden

company. She designed everything from paper plates to coffee mugs. After two years, she lost this job.

Lin took the money she received after losing her job and headed for New York City, New York. She walked up and down the city streets showing her work to anyone who would look.

Finally in 1998, an editor at a publishing company near Boston, Massachusetts, said he loved one of Lin's illustrations. It was called "The Ugly Vegetables." He asked Lin if she had a story to go with it. She did not, but she said she did! She went home and quickly put one together.

The story stemmed from Lin's own childhood. Her **botanist** mother had kept a garden of Chinese vegetables, while Lin's neighbors had grown gardens of flowers. The story tells how Lin had felt about her garden being so different from everyone else's. *The Ugly Vegetables* was published in 1999 and earned many positive reviews.

The Ugly Vegetables *includes a recipe for vegetable soup. It also gives the vegetable names in both English and Chinese.*

13

Art for a Cause

Writing and illustrating *The Ugly Vegetables* was just the beginning for Lin. Her sisters had not been in her first book, and they didn't like that! So Lin's second book, *Dim Sum for Everyone*, features three sisters. Lin also began illustrating books for other authors.

Artists created one-of-a-kind snowflakes for Lin's special project.

In June 2001, Lin married **architect** Robert Mercer. Later that year, Mercer complained of a sore muscle in his thigh. He visited a doctor to get help. Eventually, he found out he had bone **cancer**.

The next few years were challenging. Lin helped Mercer as he went through treatment for his cancer. She also continued to work on her books. Soon, the two began creating a book together.

Robert's Snow was published in 2004. It tells the story of a mouse named Robert who lives with his family in a shoe. One day during a snowstorm, Robert stays outside too long and must try to find his way back home.

To go along with the book, Lin asked 200 illustrators to create artwork on wooden snowflakes. Selling the snowflakes raised more than $100,000 for cancer research!

The snowflakes were so popular that Lin had the designs published in a book called *Robert's Snowflakes*. Money from the sales of that book also went to support cancer research. Sadly, Mercer lost his battle with cancer and died in August 2007.

A New Audience

Lin found the strength to keep going without her husband. She had been very busy during his illness. In fact, she produced three books in 2006.

One of those books was her first novel for young readers. *The Year of the Dog* is the story of a young Taiwanese-American girl named Pacy. The novel details Pacy's school and family experiences and the challenges of growing up. It takes place during the Chinese Year of the Dog, when people are meant to find their true friends.

Lin returned to Pacy's story with her second novel, *The Year of the Rat*. This story features Pacy and her friend Melody. It is based on Lin's experiences growing up with her friend Alvina Ling.

Lin met Alvina Ling (left) in junior high school. Years later,
Ling became a book editor and worked with Lin!

Writing for older readers led to a special new benefit for Lin. Before, she had received e-mails and letters from parents and teachers. Now, she began receiving notes from the readers themselves. Lin enjoys hearing from her readers. She thinks it is fun to see what questions readers have about her books.

Winning the Newbery Honor

In 2007, Lin returned to picture books with *The Red Thread*. It is a fairy tale based on a Chinese legend. The legend says that people who are meant to be together are joined by an invisible red thread. Originally, the belief applied to married couples. Lin reworked the legend to focus on the love between parents and their adopted children.

In 2009, Lin explored her Chinese roots again in her third novel. *Where the Mountain Meets the Moon* is the story of a girl named Minli. Minli leaves her home to find the Old Man of the Moon. She hopes he can help change her family's fortunes. The novel blends folktales and magical creatures inspired by Chinese stories. The result is an amazing adventure.

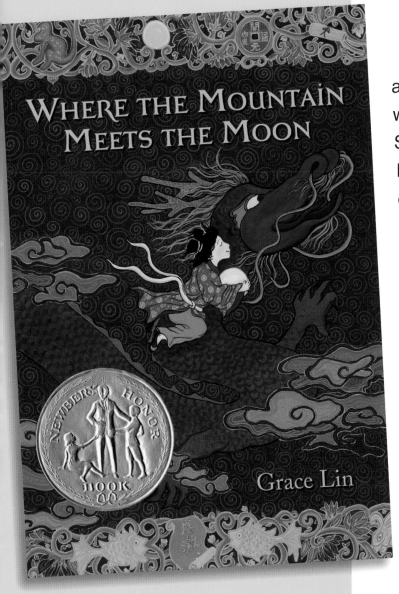

Unlike most novels, **Where the Mountain Meets the Moon** *is full of beautiful full-color illustrations. Lin and her editor fought hard to get the publisher to include them!*

Lin had written about half of the book when her husband died. She regretted that she had not finished it so he could read it. However, a friend told her it was probably good she had not finished the book sooner. If she had, she would have felt she had to keep it just the way it was. Instead, Lin could make whatever changes she needed to in the book. And after she finished it, it earned her a **Newbery Honor**. Lin was thrilled!

LOOKING FORWARD

Today, Lin lives in Somerville, Massachusetts, with her second husband, Alex. She carries a sketchbook with her at all times. She never knows when something might make her think of a new story! Lin still reads mostly children's books. Her favorites include the Harry Potter series, Beverly Cleary's Ramona books, and of course, Richard Scarry books.

Besides writing and illustrating, Lin does about 30 school visits a year. In her spare time, Lin likes shopping online, riding her bicycle, and eating desserts. She also enjoys beating her husband at video game ping-pong!

Many people love Lin's **unique** art style. It features bright, bold colors, rounded shapes, and unusual **perspectives**. There are often many special details, including swirls. Lin loves painting swirls! They are a symbol of the endless circle found in Chinese **culture**.

Lin usually works on more than one book at a time. Then if she gets stuck on one, she can move on to another for a while. She says that helps her get unstuck.

Lin tells young writers that it is important to write a story and then set it aside and write another. She remembers thinking her first story was the best story of all time. She was crushed when multiple publishers rejected it. Years later, she reread that first story. It was awful! So, Lin tells young writers to understand that what they have already written is not their best. What they write next will be better!

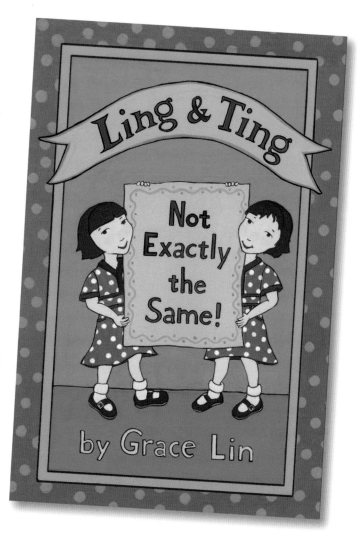

Lin's first early reader book, **Ling & Ting,** *was published in 2010. It was named a Theodor Seuss Geisel Award Honor Book in 2011.*

GLOSSARY

architect (AHR-kuh-tehkt) - a person who plans and designs buildings. His or her work is called architecture.

botanist - a scientist who studies plants.

cancer - any of a group of often deadly diseases marked by harmful changes in the normal growth of cells. Cancer can spread and destroy healthy tissues and organs.

culture - the customs, arts, and tools of a nation or a people at a certain time.

enroll - to register, especially in order to attend a school.

gouache (GWAHSH) - a method of painting with watercolors that do not let light through.

multicultural - of, relating to, or blending different cultures.

Newbery Honor Book - a runner-up to the Newbery Medal. The Newbery Medal is an annual award given by the American Library Association. It honors the author of the best American children's book published in the previous year.

perspective - the art of giving objects on a flat surface the appearance of depth and distance.

Theodor Seuss Geisel Award - an annual award given by the American Library Association. It honors the authors and illustrators of the year's best American books for beginning readers.

unique - being the only one of its kind.

WEB SITES

To learn more about Grace Lin, visit ABDO Publishing Company online. Web sites about Grace Lin are featured on our Book Links page. These links are routinely monitored and updated to provide the most current information available.

www.abdopublishing.com

INDEX